BENEATH THE HEAVY

a poetry collection by lydia falls

illustrations by james zucco

Poems in this collection have also appeared in the following publications:

Connecticut River Review
In Parentheses
The New Southern Fugitives
Sutterville Review
Train River Poetry
Unvael Journal
Yo-New York

www.lydiafalls.com
www.jameszucco.com
www.merigoldindependent.com

"And it is not yet enough to have memories. You must be able to forget them when they are many, and you must have the immense patience to wait until they return. For the memories themselves are not important. Only when they have changed into our very blood, into glance and gesture, and are nameless, no longer to be distinguished from ourselves— only then can it happen that in some very rare hour the first word of a poem arises in their midst and goes forth from them."

— *The Notebooks of Malte Laurids Brigge*
Rainer Maria Rilke

BENEATH THE HEAVY

CONTENTS

I.

SWEET VALIDATIONS

Prelude

piano fingers,
my mother called them.
long and thin
they'd dangle
self-consciously
by my sides.
there was so much of me
i learned to call
endearing.
so naturally,
i longed that
you'd learn, too.

Dead Lost Habits

my brother used to stutter, but i couldn't
keep eye contact well before it was
socially acceptable, so i was always told
an inch above the lid or a spot below
their blackened inner circles;
but now the kids are all learning from
narcissistic robots, the ones who tell time
on digital clocks, the ones who couldn't tell you
if the fifties were lived in black and white
or broken through vivid grays— and meanwhile,
my heart was groomed inside of books, two pupils
following the trail of texts along rough pages
until my eyes blurred and i had to keep dog tags
to keep track of dead lost habits
before landing on a plot
that fixed my gaze

Transient

my breath stores a secret

chilled like the fog i left
smeared on the glass

thick   and full of time

it escapes and i wonder

is this
not my   body?

we are here
in borrowed
skin

Candy Hearts

my mother reminds me
to speak like a lady
but my throat is full of
crooked terms, with a chest
prone to childish needs
of silence; i pressed my tongue
on those petty violations,
steeped in idyllic childhoods
drunk off homes outside home,
where i'd rearrange fixtures
and bathe in the void
like a sweetened treat fizzing
through acid— a candy crux
melting the mold

the voices boomed louder
as my bones shed thinner
into cages encasing all those
candy hearts, pastel and dainty,
all those sweet validations
my lacy script sore against canines—
until i'd break at the habit of
swallowing poems, of muting
my notions, and constantly
choking on words

Marked

i can't seem to find
those teeny tiny
footprints
(the ones he left
down my spine).

if i wander without
those teeny tiny
footprints,
i'll be bare-boned—
they're essential.

just give me another day
(sometime, shortly, soon).
they're teeny tiny,
those traces along my skin.
his are sure to fade.

Sensitive

they always called me sensitive,
as if flagging a flaw in red ink.
mystified
and matter of fact,
they'd pick at my scraps
like they would with worn clothes,
and it's true:

i wear a deeply
sensitive
skin.

but if they heard what i hear
as rain breaks on concrete
(our lone drops of soft grief
still echo off lost feet);
if they dreamt what i sensed
from words bent in fractions
(those petals of violet
torn swiftly
from curved trees);
if they felt what i do
beneath hollows
of half moons
(spilt stardust
from crescents
still cover
our false truths
and press in
new prints
till we bruise)—

then they would be
sensitive
too.

Projection

what do you
mean to me if not
my father

i rehearsed these lines
in shallow sleep
for days

and when startled
awake i swore
it's true

i can make a love story
out of anything

my confidence groomed
in hollowed shades
of youth

please validate me soon

II.

THIS IS OUR HISTORY

Origins

my mother
held me in her arms
when she bled

she welcomed me
in prayer

my father bowed,
heavy with gratitude

he swore to source gold
for his only daughter

stitch up sins
and sew
a sincere bloodline

so up i grew, embroidered:

subtle
nostalgic
ornate

just like

the blood they shed
the gift she bled

for home

Lydia

i blush with my middle name:
Lydia,
after my grandmother,
soft-spoken in syllables
on the street where
she rose,
a nameless named island
along seas, she resides
where my mother
calls out, still a child;
cradled in hiding
two hands whisper,
beholden, unseen:
her mother,
Lydia,
at the base of our isle,
where words become
wordless and
sounds still remain
in my seams

Five

he taught me why
bad habits
need to be broken

like my hair
unruly
unkempt

dangling down
with chewed split ends,
tangled in all my
dirty secrets

i tugged at them
in clumps of dusk
as if i could be
saved

he knew i couldn't
carry their weight
upon lips that would tighten
with age

so he took me by the wrist
pulled me to the bathroom
and chopped me some
homemade, life-
changing
bangs

it was for my own good, he declared

and so it's how i've
always worn
my hair

hushed
and full of
secrets

Green

words cling to me still
like grass on wet skin

i hated the way it felt:
the blades kicked up
all stuck
to bare feet

so those summers,
he carried me to towels
splayed across flat greens

he scooped me up
from concrete and flew me
arms spread, grinning

away from the shimmer
of pool water, thin

like the breath he held
when i cried i could
feel it again

as the dragonflies floated
he watched me
closely,

scraping the green
off my heels

For Mayor

they all cheered for my father
back in the nineties
until globs of paint
dropped from the ceiling
in buckets afloat with pride
i begged please daddy may we
take them? all of them?
a bunch of them?
a car full of them?
so we piled all that plump
empty space in the white Riviera
a back seat overflown
with those dancing balloons
stamped with bold block print and
i swam and
i swam
in their static

Uncle Tony

he always carried that strong sense
of ash; i'd smell it on his coat
the evenings he came home—
he was not my father
but my cousin's heartache.
childlike in nature, he blew up statues
and crouched in the trunk of his
pale blue pick-up, jumping out
to snatch us. we were thrown in the pool
before we learned to swim
because he swore it built up character:
always on alert, ready to flee if it saved
our lives and wouldn't we giggle so hard
when he told us tales of his teenage days,
when he would weave in our names
with his fiction.

he was mystifying: with a cask
full of words that infused all our memories
with magic. some nights, his humor kept me up
pursuing crooked branches
like the shadows freed from cornfields,
but morning always came
on Bundy Hill when i would visit;
balancing on stone walls, clutching to
the rope swing he had dangled from an oak tree,
we'd soar two stories high above a cargo truck
in the yard, and we would never wear helmets
because he swore it built up character— yet some nights,
he wouldn't come home and some days his speech
was nicked with slurred words, but the grown-ups,
all grown up, they ignored the darkness rising.

he called me before i left the country;
said he was 'kicking it in the Bronx
with a Russian fox down the block…'
just like the funny little lies,
he'd always tell me
funny little
lies…
with a sniffle of the nose,
an exhale of contrition,
with qualms still entangled in
those vanished years between us;
only moments before
the click severed our
phone ties—
muffled,
he promised
he was proud.

Where You Left Me

i walked the world without you, mostly
bumping shoulders against figures
with their chest spread open
like moths craving space, and me—
i wanted to stay small,
so i'd skip count by sevens
on tiny pink knuckles
until i landed between flaws
burrowed beneath the divots
in my ribcage

my skin sprouted beauty marks
the size of anthills,
dug up and inflamed from
carving delicate milestones
against the arches of my footprints;
i was held up by two ankles
bent from all those ages starving
collapsed into all those seasons i flinched
before touching the earth

but i will never forget it: you—
you were my first,
the long distance relationship
our parents paused their lives for,
driving miles along the reservoir,
swapping children in a parking lot
half-empty and frozen
to capture the simple way
our breath would tangle
in dusk; well this is where
you left me:

with skin stretched over
a body that begged
to be saved

Spine

my mother slid the wicked
right out of my body
she held me up with her back arched
and let the timelapse enfold:
i cracked our bloodline in half and
blew a wish right down my middle;
i crossed off freckles she painted
and hid gifts she had poured into my
piano fingers, curled over gently,
through decades outpouring
with lessons to take up more space—
it was words that fed me the most,
filled up with air like a bobble-
head knocking around
before i could center my shoulders
and exist upside down, before i broke
my own ego against a crescent-curved spine
as each notch felt the tug of the cosmos—
my mother raised me to be proud
of my insides; she drew the dusk outside
from my body, rooting my spirit
in earth

Little Gem

i was always four years behind
in motor skills and time that lapsed
between my crinkled ribs, a cage
wrapped in veins of the leaf-fall
through dry seasons, like his
aortic valve, fifteen years and
surging slightly, still taut enough
to keep his blood full of iron
as our grip stitched tight

he pierced the patch quilt mold
all stuffed with guts
like charisma
yearning to pour free...

still he cradled me and painted me
with rose, like the beautiful pillow
trimmed and sewn with the fingers
of a child, with the stutter of a kid
that spit up trust then grew holy

i envied its hem
how pretty his artwork bled
with a pristine knack
for making flaws
look golden

Milestone

he brought up the green
that used to coat my walls
like a child wailing for redemption;
i swore it was the way
i was raised (frozen from lime-
light yet still starving for
attention) and it was never
aggression i had known but
the subtleties of how words clink upon
words, striking at emboldened bones
like the keepsake of a child:
thought-struck and mesmerized
by the dull creak in knees or the
thrum beyond dusk or the
silence between dialogue (faint yet
everpresent);
                    so i took that measure
and weighed out all my paperbacks
in hopes that prose outgrows the hollow,
carving out a cold fifteen, arrested
for theft— i left the herbs in the car like
evidence seared in stone, clutching
at my notebook, grasping for the phone:
my mother is in the Philippines and
my father in the city and could we
please come to an agreement (on our
own)?
              well i could never break the spell
of birdsong, but i was told to shut my mouth
before i mispronounced my verbs
and this is where they found me: in a crinkled
plastic bag, enchanted with the mysteries that
kept me inside out; it's pistachio shells, they said—

then let me off with less, only waking to a world
where sunlight pours into a vessel like
a damp and heavy sweat, still grief-stained and
empty, grasping for regret; so later that week
i bought buckets of paint
and sloshed on
all that baby green—

the way the hue forgave me
with its teeth marks in my skin,
dull and thin yet aching,
strewn up and down my ribcage
like a milestone sculpted from bark:
burrowed in its camouflage,
yet pleading for a shade
to fill the vacant

This is Our History

he asked me to show him
where the raw is

hovering over me
like a tent in his bedroom
cluttered in the back,
his voice shook and
mine drifted, lost to a
car alarm stirring,
the light from the
lamp post, dimming
through cold glass

his imprint remained
and this is our history:
untamed, quiet
still clawing at that
long beige building
on the corner of
Valentine Lane

III.

WHERE PAST AND PRESENT MEET

A Sincere Moment

some visions are ingrained in our heads.
i was not yet seven when i set out
to combat gravity— some ride with no hands
but i just wanted to feel my in-
dependence; kiss the wind right back
on two wheels circling over an infinite halo
like a symmetry of myth. i could barely keep
my torso balanced, the weight of sunlight pulsing
through my path, so i blamed nature for the way
i crumpled with conviction, where past and
present meet— the way i manufactured
memories before they took its root in history
and i smudged the fabrication between my fingers:
the pale pink bicycle, a hand-me-down
from a junk job, or perhaps it came brand new,
two sizes too big; i grew into it half-whole yet
wobbling, so when my foot pushed the pedal
and my core felt stable, i knew spirits like these
were meant to sway off-kilter before mastering
composure and carving out a space to free
the faux from all the fiction:

to sculpt a sincere moment,
to rise up and then etch into a verse.

Nightcap

you promised to survive
when the fireflies lit up gold at dusk,
you bled out ashes when
laughter filled our
empty space,
until charcoal burnt fluff
pierced by thin bent stakes—
how the stars split so boldly,
so i counted them
softly on the car ride home,
holding each one closely,
the child i was when
the sugar rush
blitzed my veins,
when the silence
would blanket
my ache,
it was the buzz
that took you
all the way back
through our forest—
i kept your ghost with me:

your embers would
follow me
home

111 Valentine

i was barely four feet high when
Rumsey Road led us to that long beige building,
the garage, vague and ill-lit
where my soul caved in
where i watched my mother die but then wake
because dreams peeled my insides out and
god never really heard me from the darkest corner
in the coziest room at one-eleven Valentine,
off the kitchen where the light peeked in,
where i begged for our lives
a mantra i found before prayer, a breath that led me
to sleep beneath lullabies of radio-talk about
blood and then talk about death
and the terrace to my left: could they climb it?
i climbed it; i climbed into tires and out of a nest
where my heart meshed with memories
and visions leaked through:
a saturated, warm nostalgia,
a glowing heat, a glowing hue—
and my mother,
in her dark green
floral dress

Shelter

my father gathers firewood
then sets fire to the bar
by which i measure any other man;
he came at me barefooted with purpose,
cursing those childish ex-
pectations, and he calls it Peaty
like a nickname— the way it coats our throats
as he moved me back and forth, crossing oceans
just to know me, drilling my name into walls
like my addictive personality,
how it manifests in pure nostalgia
because no one would hold my bones like
he did when he shook off the grip of my
hollow, and not many people
kick it back with their folks but my father
trained his mind in the company of ghosts
and he surrendered to the void, so without
a wide-eyed blink, he kindles sun-
kissed energy into a heartfelt calm
and all those embers fall from skies
as if i'm wildly blessed and veiled
in holy fire

Honeydew

i left home with sap in my veins,
with legs like twigs
contorted from searching,
sewn into earth,
weaving through the countryside
in evanescent jade—
i missed you deeply today,
with roots firmly braided
through a bed of memories,
entrenched into leaves,
my center wrapped in branches
like a present, gathered up
and guarded from
the breeze

Ladybug

the ruby-back black spots
found me in a tent
where i sat crumbling
the sand between my iris;
i sketched the world
with a uniball pen,
knee-deep in curses against
a stubborn umbrella,
dug into my roots
as if it coils through memories
anchored in dusk-thawing drinks
of late August, as my insides
are scribed into words

afloat, i dreamt of the present:
a home to emboss you
in the paling of time and i have
searched for your forest, little one,
where the bark bursts open and
we pierce through an earth chained
to orbit; we absorb in its surface
and fiddle with grief on the outskirts
of luck, mining for ladybugs,

spiraling beside oceans, still soaring
into green, with seafoam
brimming through my eyelids—

      adrift towards autumn,
fully awake, scanning for the specks
that keep me anchored, fluttering
with ink to mark the trees

Art
in a forest

i waited for blood:
my father regretted my
shins were a canvas for scabs
the size of continents and i was a
masterpiece built for massacre: dead-
ly quiet, low in iron— pulsing with a
need to ascend, so i picked at crumbled bark
between two fingers and all the insects multiplied
on the outskirts of my flesh as if my palms came down
like a goddess; yet once i found my way around treetops
the drop felt much higher, so i made myself a home up there,
sewing leaves into my hair, reciting lines from ancient paperbacks
revived in our attic, timeless as a forest taking root inside me and i
left home with a mosaic on my body— still it's a wonder how i kept my
bones intact, and it's ironic how my sacrum fractured first along the platform
of a steel and mortar forest; had i learned nothing from my father and nothing
from the woodlands, holding nothing but a book inscribed with someone else's name?
before i could speak apologies poured out, sprouting roots to twigs, in search of affirmations
only time could pin down,   the artform of a child, still stitched along the hollows of my ribs.

Mixed Blood

i carried my insides like
an injured baby bird, clutching at
my aura with its neon light, wavering
in all those artful colors:
i leaked through waxy surfaces
of misshapen photos,
the sense of blue in lilac,
my incandescent portrait
on a melted horizontal, balanced as
i waded in the tones that washed
my world with simple truths

i stood there in stillness,
shaking off the quiet like
a wounded little girl, peeling off
the hue that grips my skin:
a composite of colors,
the blessing of mixed blood,
my words sewn into fingers
as i traced along the canvas with
a lineage distinctive, an homage
i concealed beneath unease

Jaybird

for Jay

we took off that summer on Charlesfield:
a single year between us, a playground stretched
back to where the fall would rearrange
our faintest ties into bonds built to kindle
between trees on fire
      and we were a flight risk
in search of ascension— i quietly paced
among the too-cool crowds, always unfeeling,
fiercely indifferent, and after i rambled
we obscured the restless in ashes;
i hid beneath layers of your dark beige
coat, its sleeves overgrown into wings
that would carry me over…

to all those winters on Brook Street
when frostbit evenings clung to our wrists
and you walked me towards the lamplight;
we shivered in dialogue as we leapt from house
to house and you were vaguely evanescent
when you were there but you were not,
and yet i always found your presence in
the mildest instant moment: feet clicking on the
pavement, low skies thawed overhead against
an influx of homesick, the landfall
of brilliance, we loom
and we retreat
in tandem

to all of our starburnt nights
in the violet of New England,
when you cut through cold
in springtime; i know where to find you now:
where you found me at our plummet—
i was bloody, but you loved me
now you float above
yet through me

The Unraveling

we devoured girlhood with a laugh that would
reverberate through our mothers' bones,
fought with fists dense like the flour we flung
across the kitchen counter. you lit me on fire
in a snow-ridden mess, until i swore he loved you,
he loved you not; but you still threatened those girls
who bullied me back to our childhood days,
shoveling nouns down my throat—
they seeped through my skin before
pouring out my mouth, left a crimson trail
of quiet from where i shed my veil of tough
and i ran to you smeared in their words:
the cruel crusting hard between eyelids.
i begged for mercy, shrunk myself down
at the foot of your bed, my body half-
bent, as if life were cyclic and you still
measured my insides with teaspoons,
in imperfect portions like immaculate
confetti, metamorphic dust,
the remnants of days, bound by
marrow set deeply between us

Pools of Water

i still taste chlorine in the light that presses
through my window. i was a pool rat
who shuddered at the name,
craving to be part of a sincere picture,
seven strokes beside an older brother
propelling dialogue forward with a craft
for what to say— and i,
deftly shielded from the sunlight,
eyes blind in fiction, all tripped up
and tongue-tied because words only
fit on a page. i mingled between
the shadows as if i knew the depth
that i was holding, fully engulfed in a sun-
kissed volcano, softly pulsing, itching to blow—
until my nose bled in the competition pool
and i swore it was only the pressure,
bubbles building up in the deep end.
a cold whistle twirls, shyly muffled at the cusp
of June; yet little did i know, the golden hue
was a sign: how adulthood was really child-
hood and if you count by prime numbers, slightly odd,
still left out, simply yearning to be split in two,
you could always feel senselessness
in the whiff of chemicals, how cloudy streaks
traverse through pools of water: dimly cool yet
nuanced, blurred in passing time.

Quixotic Daydreams

she reminded me of my great aunt Mildred,
yet to pass away, dining in a dim-lit corner
of Portland, Maine; she offered me her vision,
trailed me to the bathroom and i could swear
she wanted me dead; just like when my
best friend's father cut up fruit, and no man
had ever served me food, so i coughed it up
and swore i knew better: i shriveled in denial,
spit seeds on a guilt-studded plate, felt the
heavy would take me beneath covers of
quixotic colors— the drapes drew open to
drive-through nights in our white Riviera,
dinner backseat by the window, simply begging
to be seen, as i traced triads and threaded through
maroon velvet, sticky with gum stain, where i was
woven in the canopies of a cement black road and
i swore i could always make out those tail lights
like two silver eyes following me home—
they ask me why i snap, but ignore how i still count
triangles beneath my breath, and i see dead women
at restaurants order seafood, pick at fruit, and mimic
the shadows in mirrors, palms down and muddy,
smudge my lips with a tinge of red violet, fiddling
with poison, playing with lost bits between my teeth.

Through Existence

i feel the energy
of places and at times
i live life
on re-
peat

this nostalgia,
sticky like gum stain
sap

i dis-
embody
moments and
mothers become
daughters, and my father
like a brother,
well they say there's no
mistaking it, so how
do i exist?

perhaps i will always
be circling; a rhythmic loop
half here, half not,
and i can show you
how to vibrate through
existence,
        but i
could never pause
to replicate
the time

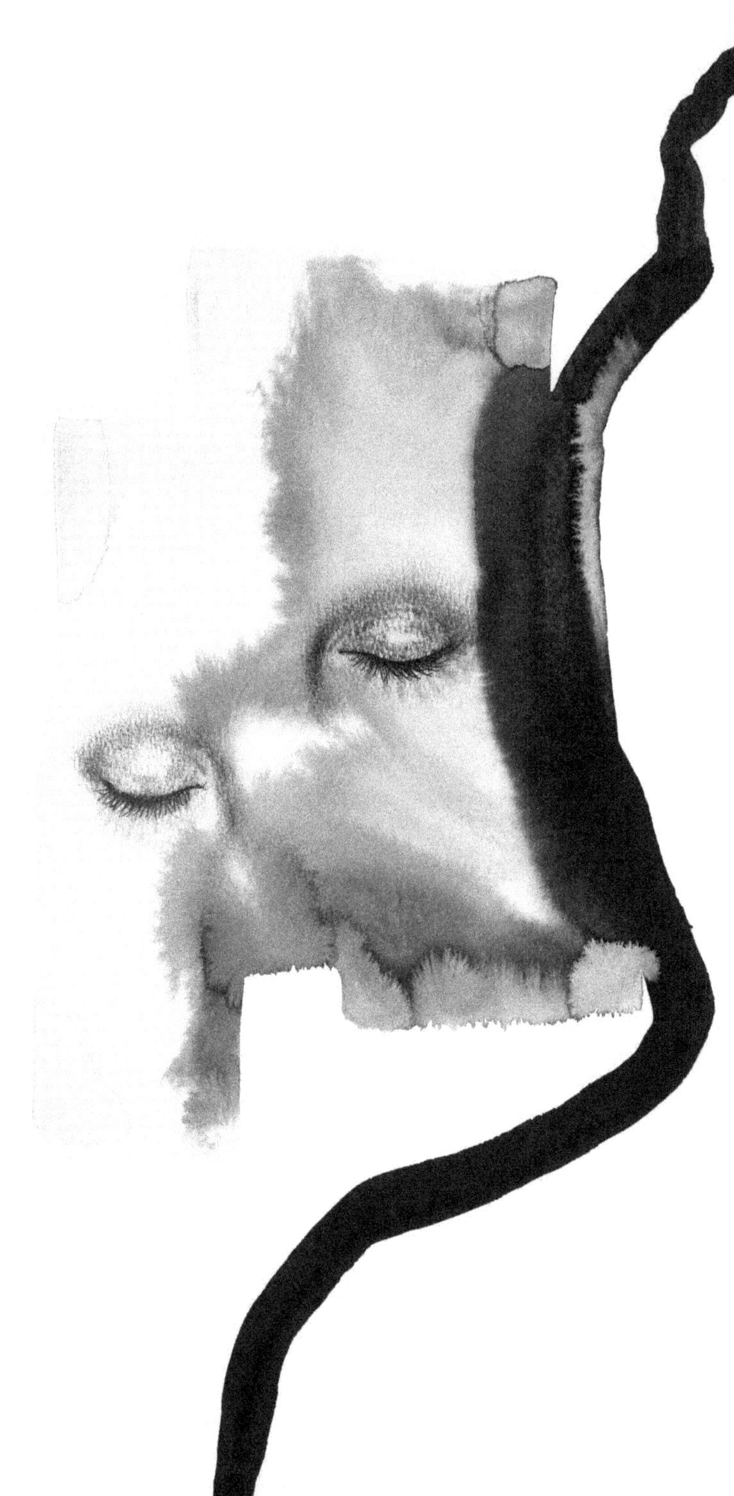

IV.

A SEASONAL SURRENDER

Self-Portrait at Dusk

my life halts when
everyone around me
seems to die and i've always
been the skinniest kind of
glutton, the one who thrives
on select attention
a specific gaze
and the way the snapshot seals
these sunken cheeks, the violet
smeared beneath
thin skin below my eyes;
how i painted them in the
darkest purple with the
saddest looking brush,
its bristles all silky yet
thinning— and you would
love my pain like you would
love to call me home
but there are times when
there are accidents or when
my life halts because everyone
around me seems to die
and i've always marveled
at the fact that my bones
are magnetic, the way they
vibrate towards ghosts
and i would never even
notice if i ceased and i would
never really know
if i had meant it

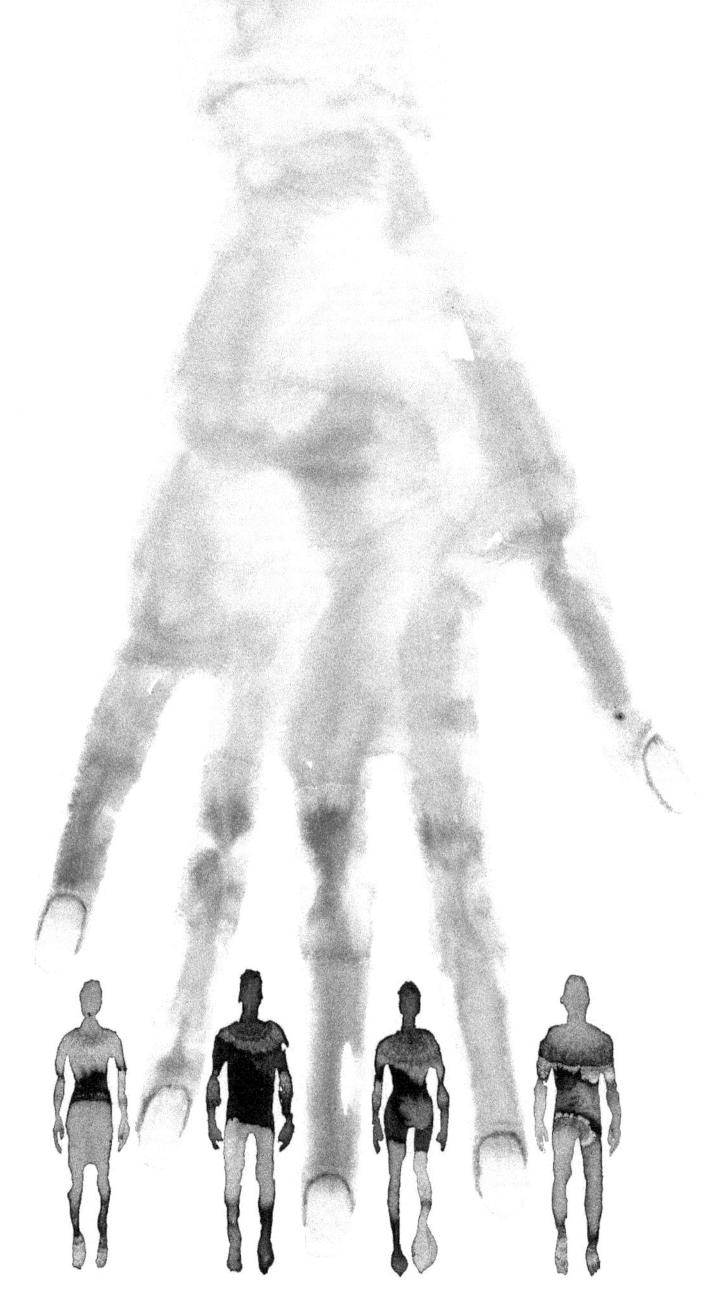

A Sense of Space

i reach out two palms
to reclaim my self:
spilling over faceless
formed to manufactured
bones, as if the tick marks
on my timeline mold to pre-
imagined blows, and i feel far

from everyone

no matter their relative position

i enlace fingers with
absence, but it is only
my lack of substance
and the inherent need
to stitch together
chronicles

of all my harbored
ghosts

The Visitation

she brought up the night we stayed
in that semi-pseudo castle in the back-
streets of Bangkok: Le Président…
El Presidencial, La Presidencia—
something slightly European, but
engraved its mark in Thailand
like a monument inscribed
in foreign tongue

she claims i haven't changed,
i haven't changed one bit,
but i explain the visitation left me
altered: i reminded her firstly
of its antiquated tiles, quaint yet
omnipresent, transitioned to
the vision that awoke me
when i slept on the cot set up
below a nook beside the kitchen

he looked at me,
face half-lit with nightlight,
unshakably tall, his body sturdy
softly unmoving,
yet astir in life, unspoken—

his neck turned with the faintest
creak to the left: taking me in,
ready to perceive me,
as if he swore i could be saved,
off-white and craving
to be seen

i relinquished beneath blankets
before i leapt out, terrified
as if a phantom writhed through me—
then she laughs; she wonders: how exactly
have you changed? and i don't fault her really,

for we never grew accustomed
to the dead

Exhumed

this is how you lose him:

with palms over-
flowing with pollin-
ating flowers filling lungs
with nonexistence like a history
embedded into soil packed in
crevices of earth sealed
with our marrow
as you leave him with
a hole carved into
spaces filled
with slumber-
weighted
words

Nightfall on Benefit Street

i couldn't tell her
where i held my shame

the library stoop
littered with grit,
crescent eyes waxed
red-eyed and ashy

through walkways
of brick,
chipped with
snow-dusted prints,
our shells wandering
vacant
for home

in rusted words
that drool from their lips
like a teardrop, twilit
wavering

toward the silent peak
of night

she drew out my insides
and i hid behind
her red pixie hair
never really questioning

if the id i purged
was foreign

Hex

he stuffed a secret
inside my balled up fist
like a desperate magician
cramming his insides into
a wooden crate because
he couldn't handle
the dire quake of manhood,
because his passion idled
and his fingers too crooked
to dig up lost doves
beneath timber

he struck at my foundation
feigning gold; before my
thoughts wove with
riddles and my bones
grew curved, his weakness
fused like molten tin
into my bloodline,
coursing through the trails
carved in my palms

so i built a crypt between
my veins, entrapping ghosts
in shameful clots,
imprinted by a secret
that was never mine
to hold

Until I Vanish

i lost you in the way of words:
speechless and confined,
you cleared your throat of the static
running up and down our timeline
while i picked daisies out of a memory bed,
seven feet deep in streams warped with coral;
i let the gravel crunch beneath my feet
as i soaked up our old patterns
in preparation for your release, and yet
you promised me, one day
we would live under-
ground and if i could only
peel off my inner psychic layers
caked and hardened to a paper-
mâchéd poem— if only i'd unbraid these
knotted verses into words for you to burn:
i am mother earth's child, half-
hallowed and imperfect with an age four crescent
floating on my chin, and if you press hard
with the rough pad of your thumb
it surely disappears, but like
a hushed pale flower
tucked quietly in my hair, i too
will furrow into ink until i vanish

Landlocked

i can contort my body into
a slew of poses, but my bones lack the
vitamin d essential for my spine to keep
from cracking beneath the pressure of
questions: like where does our conscious-
ness go when we settle back cold
into earth? well i was always scolded for my
disagreeable habit of licking open cuts
as if in adulterated lust for the taste of
human blood, the metallic force escaping
like a pulse that begs for mercy
as if it always wanted out—
the iron-laden memories
that pierce and stain
the ground
  we claim
            when landlocked hearts
expand then fold, expired

Summoned

i dreamt of your wake

your body
declining

into the silent ache of night

i held you there
as you once held me

like i could keep you
from growing
small

i begged the earth
not to take you back

not to summon
the fates
for your ashes

i swept the life
back into your bones

and you stood there

exposed in the quake
amid stratus

calling me

back home

Dangling at the Apex

if you split my life into thirds
you would have ten disheveled portions
of a full circle, as if i baked my childhood
then carved it into thirty tiny crescents the size of
pockmarks on trees, and even before we left Valentine,
i whispered trigonometry in the dark, admiring heavy colors
of crinkled leaves like the dusk in this art, and before i was
a forest girl who realized we were already dead, i gathered
dried herbs into flimsy bouquets and feigned witchcraft,
committed to dislocating stems from spines, still dangling at the apex
until i was bullied back into my skin; and there are days where i
can't even believe that was me in there, devouring my bones
for breakfast— because i believed in all those hateful things they said
and i knew what they meant when they told me all my veins
would dissolve before life could bloom
into a seasonal surrender

V.

REALIGNMENT

Birdsong

i rise low and heavy,
half-buried beneath
the wooly layers of childhood;
there is birdsong on repeat.
nostalgia is mourning
and when the dawn sets in,
memories yearn for an encore:
the minor forgivings
and vaguely missed notes
like the space between words
where floorboards still ache
with an imprint that calls out
i'm home.

An Offering

i once wandered
in the hollow

eyes heavy
on my body

childlike, shrinking

in the woods

i bowed to the earth
in half moon surrender
with a heart full of memories
my mind had released

i bloomed into spirits

aflutter
in heat

Sprigs of Lavender

the morning
breaks

breath caught calm, stirring

the way the sunlight
falls upon his face
golden

still he sleeps gently now
steeped in violet streams
of night

an unraveling
of unspeakable
beauty

in thin air
i caught him
between my daydreams

now everything
pales
in comparison

the way he gifts
my mailbox
with darkening sprigs
of lavender

Realignment

in grammar school
we lined up two by two
beside the double doors
that led into the hallway
but they never taught us
patience, so we played war games
like mercy, until a wrist snapped
and then we crafted weapons
out of spoons: we hit quarters
against each other's knuckles
until we bled out that bright
red and laughed because
that was what winning meant,
and i never really learned how
to breathe until i turned twenty-
five, displaced in a country
laced with foreign trees and
sharp winds that could whack
these branches back to
second grade and i marinated
in their calming greens
while these claws of home
came digging into my center...
with an empty sick, the dull ache
of longing— and i laughed because
my insides felt more full
when they were hollowed

Lullaby

my mind moves with my mother

her trickle of fingers
down my
       s
       p
       i
       n
       e
             chasing sleep

       be pleasant

be still,
she reminds me

smile
when eyes rest   upon me

blanket the flaws
deep be-
neath

Providence

New England made the simple promise
of following me home across
a twilight ached in chalky prints
as Transit Street swept snow
into the late mornings of
spring and some days
i'd walk home with the sun
bathing down my neck
toward a light that would beg me
for pardon—
i found out the hard way
on a mustard yellow bicycle
clinging to my skirt
like it longed for the dark
like it was built to see more
still i puttered away
along the cobblestones
of Providence
soaked in an energy
still dripping from
my knees

Acid Jeans

i used to scrunch up my soul
to the size of chewed gum
and trap that tiny sucker down
in my pockets; just take a look at
these clothes: blackened hand-
me-downs in search of ghosts,
i wore exotic like a veil of silent,
i haunted strangers who mis-
pronounced my name; i blew
bubbles in a dragonfly dress,
chasing answers like an anti-
dote to all my hallowed acid,
a trickle of guilt on repeat;
i used to apologize for all those
stains i left in dark-inked denim,
patch-quilt selves i wrapped
tightly in foil, now i wear them
like velvet, a leisurely plaid
cloaked softly with
rose-colored
seams

Bustle

from beyond
the intricate
threads
of your nest,
these crowded streets
like veins
sewn in wrists,
i look upon you
in tranquil awe;
for you have weaved
through my forest bones
and shook me

Savasana

alone has never felt lonely
stillness grips my ankles
and pulls me down to earth
so some evenings
i lie quiet
on the living room floor
as if i'm dead and vacant
replete with deep affection
as if my body served its purpose
soaked in rhythms of a heart
i vibrate, cooling hues
of violet
the tones release an energy
through verse

Legacy

i click my wrist bones
together
like two strangers
kept captive

i nosedive in friction
and curve with the depths
trapped in gaps
where i just
        can't
                        find
my voice

yet, there—
lain beneath quickened feet:
poetry in shapes

i swear i hear you there
i wear you
in my
hair
like smoke dispersed
in three thin lines
my geometric
        heaven

the words we spoke
in lost half rhymes
so softly
omnipresent

your angles   rest
     precise

my voice
still
and always
      rising

VI.

BELOW THE HORIZONTAL

Keepsake

i misplaced the light
that used to glue me to your
bedsheets; we shut the summer
outside of your porch when we
swore off all the ashes,
so i made a cave of the books you kept
and alphabetized them one
by one: counting lines that
set apart Rilke
from Rimbaud and before
the seasons ignited or i lost my face
drifting
in the violet
of a vaguely lit
sidewalk,
i tiptoed along an egg white canvas
with a backdrop half-laced like
a nest that would swallow me
whole

you rested in me and i re-
arranged the fabric, committed to your
remembrance; i ripped down all
the curtains to stitch you
a tablecloth,
ashy red— and before
you memorized my
movements, i traced over
your silhouette
with a fine tip
marker,

and now the winter shifts inside me
like a ghost, painting relics in
the margins, shadow-
tinged and whirling with
a chest that still rises in search of
an outlier— and you
beneath the shade: collecting all our
scriptures on a paperback note,
filling in my sudden loss
for words

Diversion

on our third anniversary, we were kept
apart by a lung-eating virus and a full orb,
flushed and rosy, its gravity upon us like
thirty-six decompressed petals of azalea
tucked away neatly between dot-flecked pages
where my fingers bound to words and mean-
while you drained the ink from wavering souls
until we could meet amidst these vapors in the
middle of your kitchen with a backdrop draped
in pale fake bricks, when all i could beg for was
the unknown slither of the silverfish bug
who scaled atop the box of your poems; it kept me
dangling there, forty-five degrees
below the horizontal
as i recited mathematics,
frantic for control, frenzied by
the plight to disappear

Vanishing Point

i could never let go of the awe in my bones,
so i traced figure eights above the crown of your head
as if i summoned infinity through witchcraft—
i still write you poems beneath my breath,
seven-inch fragments loop like clockwork;
until i see stars at the foot of your nest
or the nook of your den or the
floor of your shower and then dress myself
in a helium-red, spilling through the skyline
where words float away
like vivid apparitions, as if the page
were atmospheric and my ego,
once clutched tightly,
peters out into
the distance

The Distance Between

he was never supposed to leave me
but he did, in a windbreaker zipped up
to his neck; all black, too thin
for the seasons that settle into
this forest— he slung a bag over
his shoulder, dreading the trail
that stitched the distance between us
like the entrails of lost lovers
who pled to remain connected by
their insides— i was never supposed to
dig up all that earth, all the limestone had me
cracking at the knees, but i kept our story
intact, dodging tragedy with a thwack
of regret and our shoelaces, tied together,
two bunny ears bouncing along gravel
as if he had gifted me, even in departure,
dormant stirrings of life anew

Revival

he holds my head up
when my spine
caves in

across state lines
he hears me
darken

he knows my voice:
all those muted notes
coated in a damp cloak
of subtlety

like streaks of
silent
white

like lilac sprung
from dead trees

they blossom
when they
weep

The Empty Crashing

i have grown accustomed to
the way your absence
holds me

the empty crashing sideways

bubbling to our surface

the echoes rupture hushed
beneath drab sheets
encased in want

the idle
seeping
thin

muffled in our heat

the hollow roves
then settles on my
skin

The Reverence of Noise

suddenly i was not potential
but a wispy wide-eyed prospect

you blessed me with choices
and i shuddered
beneath the pollen
in a parking lot pouring
with dust

your insides were where
they were left:
unseen, undone, unfelt

so i searched myself
in the walls within your compound,
beyond the depths of my wavering frame,
feet fallen to slender zig-zags

it is there i lost my crest
in the waves of false commotion

in futures that clatter along
my centered
surface

in the moment you promised
to hold me

beneath the reverence
of noise

Apparition

i sat across you and
swore myself to secrecy.
you were only a ghost:
a phantom blessed in physical form,
a memory fluttering
towards home;
i waited half-cold and flushed
in ashes, begging for you to reveal—
to haunt me, to hold me,
to marvel at my insides carved with
prehistoric markings,
the curvature of
my indigo bones
in tender vibrations
pulling me from
the earth.

Before You Go

i asked of you the same
when we first met:
please write me a dream
i could sleep in

call it devotion—
or hopeless

i have rubbed my eyes
of the years i spent etching this earth

smeared wander with
intention, until my bones
split time
and grew home-
sick

i still vibrate with
the fear that *there*
is now

well perhaps i should
always be
floating

full of dusty
nomadic prints

before i go

please leave specks
of my skin

scattered across the hemispheres

Departure

you leave me in the wake of parting

my spirit haunts your route
until the landscape
snaps in two: nostalgia half-
contorted like a fractured
pinky promise,
my spine lain bare
and crooked across state lines,
wailing like a lost child—
calling you
back home

ABOUT THE AUTHOR

Lydia Falls is a poet and teacher who currently resides in New York. She studied Human Development at Brown University and upon graduating, received a Fulbright scholarship to teach abroad in South Korea. She returned to New York to earn her master's degree in Education at Columbia University, and then went on to teach in Taiwan for two years. Lydia's formal studies and experience living abroad in Asia further developed her interest in exploring the human psyche through poetry, yoga, and self-reflection.

ABOUT THE ILLUSTRATOR

For years, James Zucco worked as an art director in advertising. Some of his commercials are part of the permanent collection at MoMA and another was nominated for an Emmy. In 2015, craving a simpler life, James shifted his focus to fine art. He now spends his days in the studio – drawing, painting and thinking. His art resides in private collections around the world and has been featured in *The New York Times* and *The California Sunday Magazine*. James lives in Minneapolis with his wife Bethany and their dog Teddy.

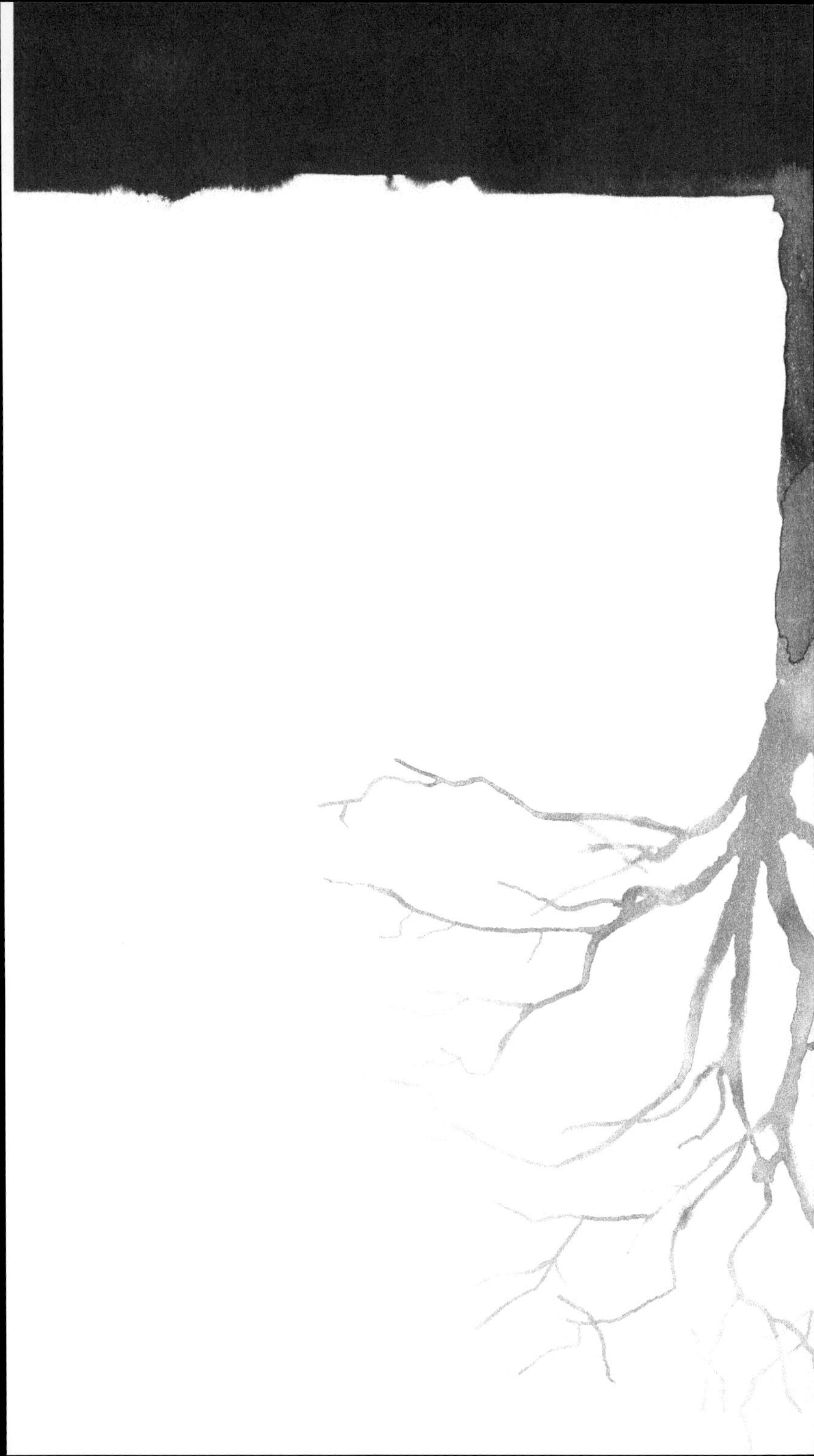

www.ingramcontent.com/pod-product-compliance
Lightning Source LLC
Chambersburg PA
CBHW050030040726
47599CB00015B/1611